SLEEP? WHAT'S THAT?

Finding Sleep at Last

Asa Eccleston Kibilski

CONTENTS

WELCOME TO THE EXHAUSTION STATION

The Sleepless Sufferer

Three A.M. The digital clock blinks a cruel reminder of my failure. I've tossed and turned, my sheets now a sweaty, tangled mess. My brain, apparently allergic to sleep, is hosting a raucous party of anxious thoughts: "What if I never sleep again?", "Can you actually die from sleep deprivation?", "Ugh, I've got that huge presentation tomorrow... Wait, was it tomorrow or Thursday?"

If this sounds familiar, welcome to the club! The Exhausted, Perpetually Haggard, I-Haven't-Slept-In-Weeks Insomniac Club. Millions of us exist, united in the misery of sleeplessness. We're the folks who can recite the ceiling patterns by heart, who've perfected the art of looking vaguely functional on three hours of broken sleep (spoiler alert: it's mostly caffeine and concealer).

You'll recognize us by the thousand-yard stare, the desperate plea in our eyes when someone says, "Just relax and you'll fall asleep!" (If only it were that simple, Karen!). We've tried every trick: warm milk (blech!), counting backward from a thousand (boring!), even meditating while imagining ourselves as a serene slug floating on a fluffy cloud (it was weird).

Insomnia isn't just about restless nights – it's the daytime too. The brain fog, the short temper, the feeling like you're wading through life in molasses. You miss appointments because you can't remember if they're Tuesday or Wednesday. You snap at your loved ones for absolutely no reason other than sheer exhaustion. The frustration builds, and the harder you try to sleep, the more elusive it becomes.

So, why this book? Because you deserve better. You deserve to feel rested, energized, and clear-headed. And while I may not have all the answers, I'm here as your fellow insomniac on this journey. We'll explore the science, the struggles, and yes, hopefully, the solutions. Buckle up, fellow sleep-deprived friends, it's time to ditch this exhaustion station and reclaim our nights!

Insomnia Defined

Okay, enough with the dramatics (for now). Let's get a little more technical about what we're actually dealing with here. The word "insomnia" gets thrown around a lot, but there's more to it than just the occasional bad night.

- **Acute Insomnia:** This is your short-term, situational sleeplessness. Maybe it's stress before a big event, jet lag, or an uncomfortable sleep environment. It sucks, but usually sorts itself out after a few days or weeks.
- **Chronic Insomnia:** This is the beast. It means difficulty falling asleep or staying asleep at least three nights a week for at least three months. This can have significant impacts on your quality of life.

Within these categories, there are more specifics:

- **Sleep Onset Insomnia:** The classic "tossing and turning for hours" situation. Your mind won't shut off and your body refuses to drift into slumber.
- **Sleep Maintenance Insomnia:** You fall asleep okay, but the problem is staying asleep. Waking up multiple times a night with the inability to fall back asleep is the hallmark of this frustrating type.
- **Early Morning Awakening Insomnia:** You know those mornings where you jolt awake at 4 AM, mind racing, and that's it for sleep? Ugh, worst feeling ever.

Now, don't stress about trying to self-diagnose. Doctors and sleep specialists are there to help with the specifics. But recognizing the general patterns is the first step in understanding what we're facing. It helps to know we're not just "bad sleepers" or somehow defective – this is a legitimate issue with real causes and potential solutions. And that, my exhausted friend, is where the journey towards better sleep begins.

WHY THE HECK CAN'T I SLEEP?!

The Usual Suspects

Let's be honest – blaming our inability to sleep on a vague cosmic conspiracy against our well-being is oddly satisfying. But for those frustrating nights when the universe seems stubbornly indifferent to your sleep schedule, it's time to play detective. There's a whole host of factors that could be sabotaging your sleep, and understanding the usual suspects is your first step toward finding some relief.

- **The Stress Monster:** The most obvious of villains. Work deadlines, relationship drama, anxieties swirling like a tornado in your head... when stress levels are off the charts, so is your cortisol – the "stay alert" hormone that has zero respect for your bedtime.

- **Caffeine: Your Favorite Enemy:** That delicious morning coffee or afternoon pick-me-up might be the very thing haunting you at night. Even if you're the type who can down an espresso and nap like a champ, caffeine has a long half-life. It lingers in your system potentially disrupting sleep hours later.

- **Revenge of the Schedule:** Your body craves consistency. If your bedtime fluctuates wildly, your circadian rhythm (your internal sleep-wake clock) throws a temper tantrum. Going to bed and waking up at roughly the same time, even on weekends, does wonders for sleep quality.

- **The Bedroom Blues:** Your bedroom should be a sanctuary, but let's be real, sometimes it feels like anything but. Too hot, too cold, too noisy, too bright... Your environment plays a huge role in whether you'll drift off easily or fight with your pillow until dawn.

- **Late-Night Snack Attack:** While a grumbling stomach

can be distracting, your midnight feasting might also be the culprit. Certain foods – heavy meals, spicy snacks – can disrupt digestion or cause heartburn, keeping you wide awake and uncomfortable.

- **The Scroll Zone:** Our beloved phones offer endless entertainment. But that blue light messes with your melatonin production (the sleepiness hormone), and the constant stimulation keeps your brain engaged when it should be winding down.
- **Booze Before Bed:** While a nightcap might make you drowsy initially, alcohol wreaks havoc on sleep quality later in the night. You might experience fragmented sleep and those dreaded early-morning awakenings.
- **Health Hijinks:** Sometimes, sleeplessness isn't just about bad habits. Chronic pain, restless legs syndrome, sleep apnea, and various other conditions can severely mess with your sleep. A doctor's visit might be in order to rule these out.

This list may feel overwhelming, but don't despair! The good news is that many causes of insomnia are within your control to change. Understanding what's keeping you awake is the key to devising a plan of attack. In the next part, we'll delve into those sneaky sleep saboteurs you might not even be aware of...

Hidden Sleep Saboteurs

If the 'usual suspects' we discussed earlier seem obvious enough, there's an entire shadowy network of sneaky villains messing with your sleep without you even realizing it. Let's expose them:

- **Light Pollution: Enemy #1:** It's not just the glaring screens in your face. Even faint sources of light – streetlights filtering through your curtains, the blinking LED on an appliance – can signal to your brain that it's time to be awake.
- **The Wrong Temperature:** Turns out, Goldilocks wasn't just picky about her porridge. Your body temperature naturally drops as you prepare for sleep. A too-warm room disrupts this process, leaving you feeling restless and sweaty. Ideal

sleep temperature? Most experts agree on a cool 60-67°F (15-19°C).

- **The Mattress Menace:** Has your mattress seen better centuries? Lumpy, saggy, or just plain unsupportive mattresses contribute a surprising amount to sleepless nights. Your body can't relax fully, and you'll find yourself tossing and turning, searching for that elusive comfortable position.
- **Sneaky Substances:** It's not just the obvious caffeine culprits. Certain medications (some for blood pressure, asthma, or even over-the-counter cold medicine) can keep you wired. Read those labels carefully!
- **Afternoon Naps: Savior or Saboteur?:** A short, refreshing nap can be wonderful... if timed correctly. Snoozing too late in the day or for too long can steal your sleep drive, leaving you wide awake when bedtime rolls around.
- **Napping Pooch (or Partner):** As much as we love them, our furry (or not-so-furry) cuddle buddies can be surprisingly disruptive. Their movements, snores, or attempts to hog the blankets might be subtly fragmenting your sleep.
- **The Worry Wart Within:** Even if you manage to put day-to-day stresses aside before bed, nighttime is prime time for the "what if..." anxieties. Your brain, unburdened by daytime tasks, suddenly fixates on existential dread or plays out a rerun of every slightly awkward interaction from the past decade.

Don't worry, identifying potential hidden saboteurs is about awareness. We can't fix what we don't acknowledge! Now that you've got a wider range of suspects in mind, it's time to get strategic in finding the culprits messing with your precious sleep.

MY BODY, MY SLEEP ENEMY

Medical Mayhem

Okay, let's get real. Sometimes insomnia isn't caused by too many late-night lattes or a bad habit of scrolling through apocalyptic news feeds before bed. Sometimes, your own body is staging a mutiny against sleep. A whole host of medical conditions can put a serious dent in your ability to get a good night's rest. Let's unravel a few of the common culprits:

- **Restless Legs Syndrome (RLS):** This neurological disorder causes an irresistible urge to move your legs, especially at night. The sensations – crawling, tingling, burning, or simply indescribable weirdness – can range from mildly annoying to downright agonizing, making it nearly impossible to fall asleep.
- **Sleep Apnea:** Dramatic snoring, huh? It might seem more like a partner problem than your own, but sleep apnea is a serious condition. You briefly stop breathing multiple times throughout the night, jarring your body awake. This fragmented sleep leads to daytime exhaustion and puts a strain on your health.
- **Thyroid Issues:** Your thyroid is the tiny, butterfly-shaped gland that acts as your body's thermostat. When it malfunctions, it can throw everything out of whack, including sleep. Both an overactive thyroid (hyperthyroidism) and underactive thyroid (hypothyroidism) can cause insomnia or disrupted sleep patterns.
- **Pain - The Uninvited Guest:** Whether it's chronic back pain, arthritis, migraines, or something else entirely, physical pain is a major roadblock to a good night's rest. It's hard to drift off when your body is constantly sending distress signals.

- **Gastrointestinal Troubles:** Acid reflux, irritable bowel syndrome (IBS), and other digestive issues don't politely clock out when you put on your pajamas. That nighttime heartburn or uncomfortable bloating can keep you awake and uncomfortable long into the night.
- **Mental Health Matters:** Depression, anxiety disorders, PTSD, and other mental health conditions often significantly affect sleep. Mood swings, racing thoughts, and heightened stress levels can lead to a vicious cycle of worsened symptoms and worsening insomnia.
- **Neurological Conditions:** Dementia, Parkinson's Disease, and other neurological conditions can directly disrupt sleep patterns. These conditions cause changes in the brain, affecting the regulation of sleep-wake cycles and causing fragmented sleep or insomnia.

This list might seem scary, but don't panic! The point isn't to self-diagnose, but rather to be aware that sometimes sleep struggles go beyond lifestyle factors. If you suspect any underlying reasons for your insomnia, a trip to the doctor is essential.

It's incredibly frustrating to feel like your body is sabotaging your sleep, but seeking professional help brings clarity and the potential for solutions. And while medical conditions present a unique challenge, they can often be managed, in turn allowing for much-needed rest.

Medication Mischief

Think your sleep battle is being fought strictly between you and your rebellious brain? There's another sneaky force to consider: the medication cabinet. Yes, the very medicines designed to help us can sometimes turn against us, messing with our precious sleep cycles. Let's delve into some common offenders:

- **High Blood Pressure Meds:** Certain medications for hypertension (like beta-blockers) can cause insomnia or vivid nightmares. The culprit could be that they slow down your heart rate, which your body then attempts to compensate for by revving up your mind.

- **Asthma Inhalers:** Albuterol, the common ingredient in many rescue inhalers, acts as a stimulant. While necessary for managing asthma symptoms, it can leave you wired and make it harder to fall asleep, especially if used too close to bedtime.
- **Antidepressants & Mood Stabilizers:** Ironically, medications aimed at improving mental health can sometimes backfire on sleep. SSRIs, SNRIs, and tricyclic antidepressants are known culprits that can cause insomnia, agitation, or restless sleep.
- **Steroids:** Prednisone and other corticosteroids are powerful anti-inflammatories, but they come with a hefty side effect – they can rev up your system and make sleep a distant dream.
- **ADHD Meds:** Stimulants used to treat ADHD naturally increase your energy levels, but the effects can sometimes linger into the evening, making it hard to wind down for bed.
- **Over-the-Counter Culprits:** Seemingly harmless stuff like decongestants (which contain pseudoephedrine) and even some pain relievers containing caffeine can disrupt your sleep more than you realize.

Now, here's the crucial part: Don't just dump all your meds in a fit of frustration! Talk to your doctor! It might be a matter of adjusting dosage, changing the timing of when you take your medication, or finding an alternative with fewer sleep-related side effects.

It's a delicate balancing act – managing your health needs while protecting your ability to sleep. The open conversation with your healthcare provider is key in finding that balance. Be your own advocate, track how different medications affect you, and keep an open mind about possible adjustments. Sometimes, small tweaks in your treatment plan can make a world of difference for your sleep.

YOUR BRAIN IS A JERK (SOMETIMES)

Racing Mind, Empty Bed

Picture this: The world is dark and quiet. It's the perfect environment for sleep, except... your brain is having a party. Thoughts bounce around like hyperactive toddlers, refusing to settle down. It's part overthinking, part existential dread, and a whole lot of "Why am I still awake?!" frustration. Let's break down why your brain turns into a relentless chatterbox come bedtime:

- **The Stress Spiral:** Remember cortisol, our favorite foe from Chapter 2? The day's stresses can leave us pumped full of this "stay alert" hormone, even when we're physically ready to crash. Your brain gets stuck in a fight-or-flight state, unable to transition to the relaxed state necessary for sleep.
- **The Revenge of Rumination:** Ever replay the same embarrassing moment from middle school, or get stuck analyzing a conversation from earlier in the day? Rumination is your brain's obsession with chewing over past events. Bedtime, unfortunately, is prime time for this mental hamster wheel.
- **Anxiety - The Unwelcome Alarm Clock:** Generalized anxiety, fear about the future, or specific worries turn your brain into a doomsday machine at night. It becomes hard to differentiate between real threats and imagined ones, leaving you wide awake with a pounding heart.
- **Hyperarousal: The Wide-Awake State:** Sometimes the root of insomnia isn't specific thoughts, but a general state known as hyperarousal. Your brain and body simply refuse to settle. Every creak of the house, every distant car alarm, jars you awake.
- **The Fear of Sleeplessness:** The more anxious we get about

not sleeping, the less likely we are to sleep. It's a vicious cycle – the pressure to perform ("I HAVE to fall asleep NOW!") backfires spectacularly, ramping up anxiety and making sleep even more elusive.

- **The Misbehaving Clock:** Our circadian rhythm, that internal sleep-wake schedule, prefers consistency. But for some of us, this clock has a mind of its own. "Delayed Sleep Phase Syndrome" means your brain naturally signals for sleep later at night and waking later in the morning. This works if your life allows it, but if you have to wake up early, sleep deprivation ensues.

Understanding *why* your brain is a jerk is just the first step. Battling the overactive bedtime mind is a multi-pronged approach. We'll delve into relaxation techniques, strategies for calming those racing thoughts, and tips for rewiring your brain's relationship with sleep in later chapters. But for now, let's just acknowledge how frustrating it is when your own mind becomes your worst enemy.

The Curse of the Night Owl

If you feel most alive and alert when the rest of the world is winding down, you might be part of the Night Owl tribe. While romanticized in literature and movies as the domain of artists and creative souls, this late-night preference can be a real source of frustration (especially when your alarm clock begs to differ). Here's the low-down on Night Owl Syndrome:

- **It's in Your Genes (Sort Of):** While not fully understood, research suggests a genetic component to your chronotype – whether you're naturally wired as an early bird, a night owl, or somewhere in between. However, environment and habits can also heavily influence your sleep-wake cycle.
- **The Misaligned Life:** Society is structured for early risers. School start times, traditional work schedules, even social events often put night owls at a disadvantage. This constant feeling of being out-of-sync can be both exhausting and

isolating.

- **The Struggle is Real:** Night owls don't choose to stay up late just to be rebellious. They often desperately try to fall asleep at "normal" hours, but their brains just refuse to cooperate. This leads to chronic sleep deprivation, daytime sleepiness, and the feeling of never being fully rested.
- **The Health Factor:** Studies suggest a concerning link between a night owl chronotype and an increased risk for health problems – from diabetes and metabolic disorders to depression and anxiety. This highlights the importance of finding ways to manage this tendency, even if you can't completely change it.

But all is not lost, my fellow nocturnal creatures! While you might not be able to magically transform into a chirpy morning person, there are strategies to cope better:

- **Strategic Light Exposure:** Bright light in the morning, and dimming lights in the evening can help signal to your brain the appropriate times for waking and sleep.
- **The Power of Routine:** As much as possible, sticking to consistent bedtimes and wake-up times (yes, even on weekends) helps regulate your internal clock.
- **Don't Fight, Negotiate:** If your schedule allows some flexibility, embrace it! Structure your day to work with your natural energy peaks rather than against them.
- **The Nap Trap:** While short, strategic naps can be useful for the sleep-deprived, as a night owl, they might sabotage your nighttime sleep even further. Proceed with caution!
- **Seek Professional Help:** If your "night owl-ness" severely impacts your life, consulting a sleep specialist is wise. They can rule out underlying conditions and help devise a plan to optimize your sleep.

The Night Owl life can feel like a constant battle. But with understanding, self-compassion, and targeted strategies, you can find ways to navigate the early-bird world and get the rest you desperately need.

SLEEP HYGIENE – WHAT'S THAT?

Habits That Haunt You

Ever heard a doctor or sleep expert drone on about "good sleep hygiene" and wanted to scream, "Just give me a magical cure already!" It may not sound exciting, but trust me, your sleep hygiene is either helping you achieve restful nights or actively sabotaging them. Let's break down what this buzzword really means:

- Sleep Hygiene: Your Routine and Environment: "Sleep Hygiene" encompasses the habits and environmental factors that influence how well (or poorly) you sleep. Think of it as the foundation of healthy sleep practices, upon which other solutions can be built.
- Beyond "Brush Your Teeth and Go To Bed": Good sleep hygiene isn't a checklist you complete ten minutes before crashing. It's about the choices you make throughout your day and how you set up your bedroom for optimal rest.

Myth Busting: Let's clear up a couple of common misconceptions:

- Myth #1: Good Sleep Hygiene = Perfect Sleep: Unfortunately, even the best sleep hygiene won't magically cure insomnia every time. Remember, medical conditions, stress, and a million other factors are at play. BUT, it gives you the best possible foundation for overcoming obstacles and getting consistent, deeper sleep.
- Myth #2: Everyone's Perfect Routine is the Same: There's no one-size-fits-all. Your ideal routine and environment will depend on your preferences, sensitivities, and lifestyle. However, some general principles form the backbone of good sleep hygiene.

So, what does bad sleep hygiene look like? Here's a glimpse:

- Erratic Sleep Schedule: Staying up late and sleeping in on weekends throws your circadian rhythm into utter confusion.
- Afternoon Caffeine Pick-Me-Up: That 4 pm latte might explain why you're staring at the ceiling hours later.
- Your Bed: Multifunctional Paradise: Working, eating, endless scrolling in bed turns it into a battleground, not a sleep sanctuary.
- Blazing Screens Until Bedtime: The blue light is your eyes' worst enemy, suppressing melatonin and sending the "stay alert!" signal.
- Bedroom = Sauna: An overly warm, stuffy bedroom disrupts the natural body temperature drop needed for falling asleep.

Feeling a little guilty? That's okay! Most of us have room for improvement. The good news is that even small changes in your habits and environment can make a significant difference in your sleep quality. In the next part, we'll get practical with tips on how to transform your bedroom into a true sleep oasis.

Bedroom Bootcamp

It's time to reclaim your bedroom as a haven for sleep... and sleep alone! Even those of us who love curling up in front of the TV or answering emails from bed need to understand that these activities are confusing our brains. The goal is to create an environment so strongly associated with sleep, relaxation, and *only* those things, that your body begins to unwind the moment you step inside. Here's how:

- The Power of Darkness: True, blackout-level darkness is ideal. Even small sources of light can disrupt melatonin production. Invest in blackout curtains, eye masks, and cover any annoying blinking LEDs from electronics.
- Cool & Comfy: Aim for a bedroom temperature between 60-67°F (15-19°C). Adjust to your comfort, but fight the urge to snuggle under piles of blankets. Your body needs to

cool down for optimal sleep.

- Banish the Noise: The quieter, the better. If you're sensitive to noise, consider a white noise machine or earplugs to block out distracting sounds. Even subtle disturbances like a ticking clock or humming refrigerator can disrupt your sleep.

- Mattress Matters: It's the foundation (literally!) of good sleep. If yours is more battlefield than peaceful retreat, it might be time for an upgrade. Experiment with different firmness levels and materials to find what truly supports your body.

- Pillow Talk: Don't underestimate the power of the right pillow. Neck pain, misalignment, and even snoring can result from the wrong pillow. Find a shape and fill that aligns with your sleep position and personal preference.

- Bedding Bliss: Choose breathable, natural fabrics – think cotton or linen. Silky sheets might feel fancy but can make you hot and sweaty. Textures matter too, so find what feels both comforting and conducive to sleep for you.

- Goodbye Gadgets: Resist the temptation! Phones, tablets, laptops – their screens and their stimulating content have no place in the bedroom. If you must use them, implement "screen curfew" at least an hour before bed.

- The Scent of Serenity: Subtle scents like lavender can have a calming effect. Use essential oils in a diffuser, a pillow spray, or try an eye mask infused with calming scents.

- A Clutter-Free Zone: A chaotic bedroom equals a chaotic mind. Limit clutter, keep surfaces clear, and consider creating a designated 'relaxation corner' for activities like reading or meditation

Remember, it's about creating a space with a singular purpose: sleep. This may take some adjusting, and don't aim for perfection overnight. Even small changes can yield big improvements. Start with the elements most disruptive to *your* sleep and experiment to find your perfect sleep sanctuary formula.

RELAX... HOW THE EFF DO I DO THAT?

Stress, the Sleep Wrecker

We know stress is the villain in this bedtime story. Daytime anxieties seeping into the night, cortisol coursing through your veins, and your mind buzzing like an angry mosquito – this doesn't exactly pave the way for the Land of Nod. But just knowing stress messes with sleep isn't enough. Let's unravel the science behind *why* and *how* your jumbled nerves ruin your rest:

- The Primal Response: Remember that "fight-or-flight" state? Stress triggers an evolutionary response designed for survival in the face of immediate danger. Your heart races, breath quickens, muscles tense – all meant to help you outmaneuver that saber-toothed tiger. Not so useful when the perceived "threat" is an overflowing inbox or a looming deadline.
- Cortisol: Public Enemy #1: This stress hormone is vital in the right context. It boosts energy in the morning and helps us face challenges. But chronically elevated cortisol wreaks havoc on sleep. It disrupts your circadian rhythm, making it harder to fall asleep and stay asleep.
- Sleep, Interrupted: Stress-induced hyperarousal means your brain and body struggle to reach the deep, restorative sleep stages. You might wake frequently, have vivid or disturbing dreams, and feel groggy even after a seemingly "full" night's sleep.
- Mental Mayhem: Stress feeds anxiety, anxiety fuels insomnia, and insomnia magnifies stress. It's a vicious cycle, and it's not just about the *moment* you try to sleep. The anticipation and dread of another sleepless night further perpetuates the problem.

- The Weakened Defense: When you're constantly running on stress and adrenaline, your immune system takes a hit. This makes you more susceptible to physical illnesses, which – you guessed it – can further disrupt your sleep! It's a nasty downward spiral.

Is the picture getting bleak? Don't despair! While stress is a formidable foe, it's not invincible. It's crucial to recognize the stress-sleep connection as the first step in breaking free from its clutches. In the next part, we'll introduce some tools to tame your stress monster and pave the way for truly restful nights.

Your Chill-Out Toolkit

Telling yourself to "just relax" when you're feeling overwhelmed is like telling a hurricane to simmer down. It's infuriating and useless. But finding relaxation techniques that resonate with you is a powerful weapon in the fight against insomnia. Think of it as building a toolbox of calming practices you can call upon when tension strikes. Let's explore a few options:

- Deep Breathing: Simple yet potent. Focused breathing exercises activate the parasympathetic nervous system, counteracting the "fight-or-flight" response and lowering your stress levels. Experiment with techniques like belly breathing, 4-7-8 breathing, or alternate nostril breathing.
- Mindfulness & Meditation: The art of present moment awareness can be life-changing. It's not about "emptying your mind" (that's impossible!) but about noticing and accepting your thoughts and feelings without judgment. Guided meditations, mindfulness apps, and even simple body scans are amazing starting points.
- Progressive Muscle Relaxation: Tensing and gradually releasing muscle groups across your body teaches you to identify and release physical tension. It's an effective way to combat that tight, wired feeling and promote full-body relaxation.
- The Power of Visualization: Imagine yourself in a peaceful

setting: a quiet beach, a lush forest... engage your senses. Studies show that guided imagery can reduce stress and induce a sense of calm. You can find guided visualizations online or simply create your own mental escape.

- Gentle Movement: Yoga, tai chi, or even a relaxing walk in nature combine physical activity with mindfulness. Movement can help release pent-up stress and cultivate a sense of calm within the body.

A Word on Awkwardness: Don't be put off if these techniques feel strange or forced at first. It takes practice! Start with short sessions (even 5-10 minutes is beneficial) and gradually increase the duration as it becomes more comfortable.

Important Notes for Insomniacs:

- Don't stress if it doesn't "click" immediately: Find what works for you. If guided meditations leave you frustrated, try gentle music or nature sounds. Everyone is different!
- Timing Matters: While relaxation techniques are amazing, doing them right before bed might be counterproductive for some. Try building them into your day to lower your overall stress level, making relaxation at bedtime easier.
- It's Not A Magic Bullet: Relaxation doesn't erase problems, but it builds greater resilience. You'll still have stressful days, but with tools to manage how stress affects your body and mind, sleep becomes less vulnerable.

Relaxation is a skill. The more you practice, the easier it gets, and the more profound the benefits for your sleep and overall well-being.

WHEN COUNTING SHEEP TURNS VICIOUS

The Frustration Spiral

Imagine this: You've tried all the "right" things. The room is dark, cool, and gadget-free. You've even done relaxing yoga earlier in the evening. But as your head hits the pillow, it begins: the relentless mental chatter, the anxiety about *not* sleeping, and the growing frustration with each passing hour.

This isn't just about having trouble falling asleep; this is when the very act of *trying* to sleep becomes the enemy. Let's break down this unique kind of insomnia misery:

- Performance Anxiety in Bed: The harder you try to fall asleep, the more elusive it becomes. Focusing intensely on making sleep happen backfires spectacularly, leaving you stressed, anxious, and wide awake.
- Fear Takes Hold: Anxiety about sleeplessness turns into full-blown dread before bed even rolls around. The anticipation of failure creates a self-fulfilling prophecy, making insomnia inevitable.
- Obsessing over Time: Clock watching is a special kind of torture. "It's 3 AM... I only have four hours until my alarm... I'll be a wreck tomorrow!" Every minute magnifies the feeling of desperation.
- Hyperarousal in the Spotlight: When you're fixated on not sleeping, your body becomes hyper-aware of every sensation. The slightest creak, your own心跳, even the feeling of your sheets suddenly seem jarring and disruptive.
- Negative Thought Loops: "I'm never going to sleep again" "This is ruining my life" "I'm going to lose my mind" Your brain transforms into a relentless critic, deepening your

anxiety and making sleep seem impossible.

So, you lie there, exhausted but enraged, feeling utterly helpless and trapped in your own wakefulness. This creates a vicious cycle – the more frustrated and anxious you feel about *not* sleeping, the less likely you are to sleep.

Breaking this spiral isn't easy, but it's absolutely essential for reclaiming your nights. In the next part, we'll explore counterintuitive solutions and mindset shifts to combat this sleep-sabotaging cycle.

Breaking the Cycle

When you're stuck in the frustration spiral, conventional advice often makes things worse. Telling yourself to "relax" or "think positive thoughts" becomes a cruel joke. This struggle needs an alternative approach. Here are some strategies to change your relationship with sleeplessness:

- Acceptance (Yes, Really!): It sounds counterintuitive, but accepting wakefulness can lessen its power. Instead of fighting against it, try saying, "Okay, I'm awake now, it's uncomfortable, but I can handle this." Acceptance breaks the cycle of struggle and lessens the anxiety fueling your wakefulness.
- Get Out of Bed (Temporarily): Tossing and turning, getting increasingly frustrated, trains your brain to associate your bed with anxiety, making the problem worse. If you haven't fallen asleep within roughly 20-30 minutes, get up for a while. Do something calming like reading a book in dim light or having a cup of herbal tea, then return to bed only when you feel drowsy.
- Reframe Your Thoughts: Challenge those negative, catastrophic thoughts. Remind yourself, "This is temporary, lack of sleep is uncomfortable but not dangerous, and I've gotten through tough nights before." It doesn't magically make you fall asleep, but it lessens the emotional turmoil.

- Mindfulness in the Moment: Instead of dwelling on the past or future, focus on the here and now. Notice the feeling of the bed beneath you, the rise and fall of your chest, the sounds around you. This gentle anchoring technique can bring a surprising sense of calm.
- "Paradoxical Intention": This technique involves embracing wakefulness, even welcoming it. Tell yourself, "I'm going to stay awake as long as possible". This counterintuitive approach sometimes reduces performance anxiety and allows for sleep to sneak in.
- Don't Expect Perfection: The goal with these strategies isn't to immediately fall asleep every time. It's about reducing the distress caused by the frustration spiral. Even small improvements make a difference in breaking the cycle long-term.
- Seek Professional Help: If these techniques aren't enough, Cognitive Behavioral Therapy for Insomnia (CBT-I) is highly effective. A therapist will guide you through addressing unhelpful thoughts, habits, and sleep behaviors.

Changing your relationship with wakefulness is not easy, and it takes patience and practice. But by lessening the fear and frustration fueling your insomnia, you break a powerful cycle, paving the way for calmer, more restful nights – even if they don't come immediately.

REVENGE OF THE TECH

Screens: The Sleep Stealers

In the modern world, screens have become nearly inescapable. They are our entertainment, our connection to the world, and sometimes, our entire livelihoods. But here's the harsh truth: that glowing blue light from your devices is messing with your sleep big-time. Here's how:

- Melatonin Mayhem: Melatonin is your body's natural "sleepiness" hormone. It starts rising a few hours before your usual bedtime, signaling that it's time to wind down. However, the blue light emitted by screens suppresses melatonin production, essentially tricking your brain into believing it's still daytime.

- Circadian Rhythm Confusion: Your circadian rhythm, that internal sleep-wake clock, loves consistency. Exposure to bright light in the evening sends wrong signals, shifting your clock later. This makes it harder to fall asleep at your desired time and might leave you waking up groggy even after sufficient hours of sleep.

- Mental Stimulation Overload: Even if you're watching something "relaxing" before bed, your brain stays engaged. Social media scrolling, addictive games, or doom-scrolling news feeds send your mind into overdrive, making the transition to sleep incredibly difficult.

- The "Just One More..." Trap: It's so easy to fall into the trap of "just one more episode", "just one more level", "just one more article." This further delays sleep onset and compromises your overall sleep duration.

- The Bedroom Invader: Even if you turn off the big screens, your phone remains a temptation. Late-night notifications, the urge to check emails, or just mindlessly scrolling disrupt sleep even if you fall back asleep quickly.

The consequences of tech-induced sleep disruption go beyond simply feeling tired:

- Daytime Blues: Poor sleep translates to daytime sleepiness, irritability, difficulty concentrating, and a greater risk of accidents.
- Health Worries: Chronically disrupted sleep increases your risk for a whole host of problems including obesity, diabetes, heart disease, and even some forms of cancer.
- Mental Struggle: Sleep deprivation worsens mood disorders like anxiety and depression, making it even harder to cope.

Does this mean you have to go full-blown Amish? Not necessarily. But awareness of tech's impact on your sleep is the first step towards forging a healthier digital relationship. In the next part, we'll discuss how to create a sleep-friendly tech routine.

Digital Detox

You don't have to ditch technology entirely to protect your sleep. Instead, it's about establishing boundaries and implementing healthy tech habits. Here's how to create a digital detox plan:

Start with the "Screen Curfew": Decide on a non-negotiable time when screens go off each night – ideally at least one hour, but preferably two or more, before bed. Stick to this religiously, even on weekends, to let your brain adjust to reduced light exposure.

Create a Charging Station... Outside Your Bedroom: Fight the temptation to scroll in bed by designating a place for your devices to "sleep" overnight. Leaving them out of sight lessens the urge to mindlessly pick up your phone and sabotage your sleep.

Embrace the Power of Dimming: Many devices offer "night mode" or adjustable screen warmth. This reduces the blue light intensity, lessening the impact on melatonin. Also, lower the overall brightness of your screens in your evening hours.

Rethink Your Entertainment: Swap late-night Netflix binges with activities that promote relaxation. Reading (a physical book!), listening to calming music, or taking a warm bath create a much better transition into sleep mode.

Beware of "Revenge Bedtime Procrastination": If you find yourself staying up late engrossed in your phone simply because it feels like the only "me-time" you get, this signals a larger issue. Prioritize some non-screen time for yourself throughout the day to combat this sleep-sabotaging pattern.

Use Apps Wisely: Ironically, some apps can help with your digital detox. Timers that shut off access to distracting apps, apps that gradually dim your screen in the evening, or ones tracking your screen time can be useful tools, provided they don't become just another reason to look at your phone!

The Transition is Key: Abruptly going from screen time to lights off can be jarring. Create a wind-down routine in the hour before your "screen curfew". Dim the lights in your home, engage in calming activities, and allow your brain time to transition to sleep mode.

It's okay if it's difficult at first! Old habits are hard to break, and the lure of our devices is strong. Don't be discouraged by slip-ups – simply acknowledge them, and recommit to your digital detox plan. With time and perseverance, you'll retrain your brain to associate evenings with relaxation, not with glowing screens, setting the stage for more restful, rejuvenating sleep.

DIET: FUEL OF DREAMS OR NIGHTMARES

The Food, Mood, Sleep Connection

We tend to think about food and sleep as separate entities. But the truth is, what you put in your body throughout the day, and especially in the hours leading up to bedtime, can significantly impact how well you sleep at night. Let's unravel the complex interplay between diet, mood, and sleep:

The Gut-Brain Axis: Your gut houses trillions of bacteria, collectively known as your gut microbiome. This isn't just about digestion! Research shows that your gut microbiota plays a role in regulating mood, stress response, and even the production of sleep-promoting neurotransmitters. An unhealthy gut can send messages to your brain that trigger anxiety, low mood, and ultimately, difficulty sleeping.

Blood Sugar Rollercoaster: Eating sugary snacks, refined carbs, or large, heavy meals too close to bedtime causes spikes and crashes in your blood sugar. This leads to nighttime awakenings, restless sleep, and vivid dreams. Moreover, consistently poor dietary choices over time can lead to insulin resistance, which is linked to a higher risk of sleep disorders.

Caffeine's Hidden Hangover: Your afternoon latte or even that dark chocolate square after dinner could be sabotaging your sleep. Caffeine lingers in your system for a long time, interfering with deep sleep stages even if you don't feel jittery.

The Alcohol Deception: While a nightcap might make you feel drowsy initially, it leads to fragmented sleep with frequent awakenings later in the night. Alcohol also disrupts REM sleep, the stage essential for memory consolidation and emotional processing. You might get your hours in, but wake up feeling far from rested.

Nutritional Deficiencies: Not getting enough of certain nutrients, like magnesium (involved in muscle relaxation) or vitamin D (linked to better sleep regulation), can subtly impact your sleep quality. While a healthy diet cannot cure insomnia on its own, it plays a crucial supporting role in optimizing your body's ability to rest.

Late-Night Snack Attack: Eating too close to bedtime, especially large or heavy meals, can disrupt digestion, causing heartburn, bloating, and discomfort that prevent you from falling asleep. A growling stomach is equally disruptive, and waking up with hunger pangs can make falling back asleep difficult.

It's not about deprivation or rigid rules! A healthy relationship with food promotes both physical and mental well-being, setting the foundation for better sleep. In the next part, we'll explore practical tips for making sleep-friendly food choices.

Hunger Games at Midnight: Strategies for Dealing with Nighttime Cravings & Improving Sleep

Knowing how food impacts sleep is half the battle. Now, let's get tactical, especially when those nighttime cravings hit hard. Here are strategies for mindful eating to promote better sleep:

Dinner Timing Matters: Eating a balanced dinner with protein, healthy fats, and whole grains a few hours before bed allows for proper digestion and stable blood sugar levels throughout the night. Avoid late, heavy meals that could lead to discomfort and disrupted sleep.

Mindful Snacking: If you absolutely must snack before bed, make it strategic. Choose options that promote sleepiness, like a small bowl of oatmeal with banana (both provide tryptophan, involved in melatonin production), yogurt with berries, or a handful of nuts.

Beware of Hidden Triggers: Take note of specific foods that cause indigestion, heartburn, or leave you feeling overly energized at night. Everyone's sensitivities vary, so personalize your "avoid" list for better sleep.

Hydration is Key: Dehydration can masquerade as hunger sometimes. Sip on water throughout the day and have a glass with your evening snack. Rule out thirst before reaching for food you might not actually need.

Break the Emotional Eating Cycle: If boredom, stress, or anxiety trigger nighttime snacking, it's crucial to address the root cause. Practice relaxation techniques, have a calming bath, or journal instead of turning to food for comfort.

Plan Ahead: Having sleep-friendly snacks prepped makes healthy choices easier when cravings hit. Think sliced fruit, pre-portioned nuts, or whole grain crackers with cheese. This prevents mindless munching on something less-than-ideal out of desperation.

Don't Ditch Breakfast!: Starting your day with a balanced breakfast helps regulate blood sugar and hormones, reducing the likelihood of ravenous late-night cravings that can sabotage sleep.

Beyond Individual Foods: Focus on an overall healthy, balanced dietary pattern. Whole, unprocessed foods, plenty of fruits and vegetables, and adequate protein throughout the day support both physical and mental well-being, naturally promoting a healthier sleep cycle.

Listen to Your Body: Learn to recognize true hunger cues versus emotional urges to eat. Pay attention to how your body feels after eating certain foods and make adjustments based on your individual response.

Remember, this isn't about perfection. Slip-ups happen! Focus on making gradual, sustainable changes that improve both your daytime energy levels and your sleep quality. Even small improvements can make a significant difference over time.

EXERCISE: TO SWEAT OR TO SLEEP?

Timing is Everything

We know exercise is good for us. But its relationship with sleep is a bit more nuanced. Getting your sweat on can definitely improve sleep quality, but it's crucial to get the timing and type of exercise right. Here's the lowdown on how physical activity can help – or hinder – your sleep:

The Benefits: Let's start with the good news. Regular exercise:

- Improves Sleep Deeply: Moderate-intensity exercise increases the time you spend in deep sleep – the most restorative stage. This makes your sleep more efficient, leaving you feeling more refreshed upon waking.
- Reduces Stress & Anxiety: One of the main ways exercise helps sleep is by easing stress and those racing nighttime thoughts. Physical activity helps burn off excess cortisol and promotes the release of feel-good endorphins.
- Provides Natural Tiredness: Expending energy during the day creates a natural need for rest at night. It's a much healthier way to induce sleepiness than relying on sheer exhaustion from insomnia.
- Helps With Timing: Regular exercise strengthens your circadian rhythm. This means your body becomes better at recognizing the appropriate times for sleep and wakefulness, aiding natural sleepiness at bedtime.
- Potential Benefits for Restless Legs & Sleep Apnea: While not a cure-all, exercise can reduce the severity of Restless Legs Syndrome symptoms and may play a role in managing sleep apnea for some individuals.

Timing the Trouble: Despite the benefits, exercising too close to bedtime can backfire, Here's why:

- Elevates Your Energy: Vigorous exercise increases your core body temperature, heart rate, and adrenaline levels. This wakes you up – the opposite of what you need for falling asleep!
- Delays Melatonin Release: Bright lights common in gyms and the mental focus of strenuous workouts can suppress melatonin production in the evening, making it harder to wind down for bed.
- Over-Exhaustion: Feeling completely wiped out after a late workout might seem like a ticket to sleep paradise, but sometimes overtraining can leave you feeling wired and restless, making sleep difficult.

This doesn't mean you should ditch your workouts! Exercising at the right time can be a powerful ally for better sleep. In the next part, we'll delve into strategies for maximizing the sleep benefits of your fitness routine.

Sleepy Workouts

Harnessing the power of exercise for sleep requires some strategic planning. Here's how to ensure your workouts enhance, not hinder, your rest:

The "Sweet Spot" Timing: For most people, the best time for sleep-friendly workouts is in the morning or afternoon. This allows your body temperature and energy levels to return to normal before bedtime. However, everyone's internal clock is slightly different – experiment to find what works best for you.

The Workout Wind-Down: Regardless of when you exercise, prioritize a cool-down period. Spend a few minutes on gentle stretching or light activity to help your heart rate and body temperature lower gradually. This signals to your body that it's time to transition to relaxation mode.

Respect the Three-Hour Rule: As a general guideline, try to finish moderate or vigorous workouts at least three hours before your desired bedtime. This gives your body enough time to wind down and prepare for sleep onset.

Embrace Gentle Evening Movement: If you only have time for workouts in the evening, it doesn't mean doom! Opt for calming activities like yoga, light stretching, or a leisurely walk. These promote relaxation and can be beneficial for sleep.

Listen To Your Body: Pay attention to how your body responds to exercise at different times of day. If a late-night run keeps you buzzing for hours, it's time to switch your schedule. Some flexibility around your fitness routine is sometimes necessary to protect your sleep.

Be Mindful of Light: If you exercise outdoors or in a brightly lit gym in the evening, consider reducing your light exposure afterward. Dim the lights in your home and minimize screen time to enhance a sleepy atmosphere.

Consistency is Key: Regular exercise has the most profound impact on your sleep patterns. Aim for consistent moderate-intensity workouts most days of the week. Even a short brisk walk is better than no activity.

Don't Force It: On those nights when you're already exhausted and struggling with insomnia, skipping your workout in favor of rest might be the better choice. Pushing yourself too hard can exacerbate sleep problems in the long run.

A Word on Sleep Disorders: If you have a diagnosed sleep disorder, it's essential to consult your doctor about an exercise plan. They can advise you on the best types of exercise, ideal timing, and how to navigate any specific considerations regarding your condition.

Remember, exercise is a valuable tool in your sleep arsenal, but it's only one part of the picture. Combining a strategic exercise routine with good sleep hygiene habits and addressing any underlying anxieties or medical conditions will lead to the most significant improvements in your sleep quality.

NATURE'S LITTLE HELPERS

Supplements & Such: Examining the Evidence (or Lack Thereof)

With the dizzying array of pills, teas, and tinctures claiming to cure insomnia, it's tempting to seek a quick fix in a bottle. But before you dive into the world of sleep supplements, it's crucial to separate marketing hype from scientific reality. Let's examine some common over-the-counter sleep aids and the evidence behind them:

Melatonin: The Star with Mixed Reviews: Melatonin, the sleepiness hormone our body naturally produces, can be effective in certain situations. It's helpful for shift work sleep disorder, jet lag, and some cases of delayed sleep phase syndrome. However, for general insomnia, it's not the cure-all it's often advertised as. Dosage, timing, and individual response matter significantly.

Chamomile: Mild Relaxation, Unclear Sleep Impact: Known for its calming properties, chamomile is often found in sleepy-time teas. While it might induce relaxation, studies on its direct effect on insomnia are limited and show mixed results.

Valerian Root: Dubious Claims: Despite its popularity, research on valerian root's effectiveness for insomnia is inconsistent. Some studies suggest a small benefit, while others show none. More research is needed to fully understand its potential.

Magnesium: A Supporting Role: Magnesium deficiency can contribute to muscle tension and restless legs, potentially disrupting sleep. If you are deficient, supplementation might help, but it's not a guaranteed insomnia fix.

L-theanine: Promotes Calm, Not Necessarily Sleep: This amino acid found in tea may reduce anxiety and promote relaxation. It might indirectly aid sleep for some, but shouldn't be relied upon as a primary insomnia treatment.

The Risks to Consider:

- Not a Substitute for Good Sleep Habits: Supplements should never replace addressing the root causes of insomnia. They may work temporarily, but they don't teach you the skills needed for long-term sleep improvement.
- Lack of Regulation: The FDA doesn't regulate supplements with the same rigor as prescription medication. Quality, purity, and potency can vary between brands.
- Interactions are Possible: Some supplements can interfere with medications you're taking or worsen underlying health conditions. Always talk to your doctor before trying any new sleep aid.
- Side Effects Happen: Even seemingly natural supplements can have side effects. Digestive upset, headaches, and morning grogginess are possible.

It's important to manage expectations. Supplements might provide a slight edge for some, but for many, their impact on sleep remains questionable. In the next part, we'll discuss the potential of herbal remedies and the importance of a healthy dose of skepticism.

Herbal Allies?

The realm of herbal sleep remedies is vast and often relies on anecdotal evidence. While some plants may have calming or sedative properties, it's essential to approach them with caution and a critical eye.

Commonly Used Herbs for Sleep:

- Lavender: The scent of lavender is often touted for its relaxation benefits. While it may create a calming ambiance, its direct impact on sleep remains scientifically unclear. Limited research suggests it may be mildly beneficial when used in aromatherapy.

- Passionflower: Traditionally used to ease anxiety, it has some scientific backing as an anxiety reducer, but its impact on sleep itself is less well-established.
- Lemon Balm: A member of the mint family, it is thought to promote relaxation. However, studies on its direct effect on sleep are limited.
- Kava Kava: This herb has been the subject of serious safety concerns and is not recommended due to a potential risk of liver damage.

Important Considerations:

- Lack of Rigorous Studies: While some herbs show preliminary promise, well-designed, large-scale studies on their effectiveness for insomnia are often lacking.
- Individual Variability: Just like with any medication, individuals respond differently to herbs. What works for one person may do nothing for another, or even cause adverse reactions.
- Safety Concerns: Herbs can interact with medications, worsen existing health conditions, or have unanticipated side effects. Their "natural" status does not guarantee safety.
- Quality Matters: Herbal preparations aren't subject to the same regulation as medications. Dosages and ingredients can vary widely, making it difficult to know what you're actually getting.

A Healthy Dose of Skepticism: Don't be fooled by testimonials or slick marketing. Remember, companies selling herbal sleep aids profit from your desperation for better sleep. Always research extensively and approach claims with critical thinking.

When is a Professional Opinion Needed?

- Before Taking Any Herb: This is especially crucial if you have underlying health conditions, take any medications, or are pregnant or breastfeeding.
- If You Experience Side Effects: Herbs can cause allergic

reactions, digestive upset, or more serious side effects. Seek medical advice if you experience anything concerning.

- If Sleep Issues Worsen: Herbs aren't a cure for insomnia. If your sleep struggles continue or worsen, seek professional help to address the underlying causes.

While it's tempting to seek quick fixes, sleep solutions marketed as "natural" should never be assumed risk-free. Your doctor is the best person to guide you on whether a particular supplement or herb is safe and appropriate for your individual circumstances.

DO I NEED PROFESSIONAL HELP?

Therapy to the Rescue: Explain Cognitive Behavioral Therapy for Insomnia (CBT-I)

When insomnia feels like an unbeatable foe, the frustrating cycle of sleepless nights can lead to a sense of hopelessness. The good news is, help is available, and one of the most effective treatments doesn't involve medication at all. It's time to introduce CBT-I: Cognitive Behavioral Therapy for Insomnia.

CBT-I: More Than Just Talk Therapy: This structured treatment specifically targets the thoughts, behaviors, and habits that perpetuate insomnia. It's a multi-pronged approach that involves working with a sleep therapist over several sessions to:

- Unravel Negative Thought Patterns: CBT-I helps you identify and challenge the unhelpful thoughts and beliefs about sleep fueling your anxiety. You'll learn techniques to replace catastrophic thinking with more realistic and calming perspectives.
- Change Sleep-Sabotaging Behaviors: This might involve adjusting sleep timing, getting out of bed when you can't sleep, limiting naps, and creating a consistent sleep routine. You'll learn to re-associate your bedroom with sleep and relaxation.
- Techniques for Relaxation: CBT-I often involves learning relaxation strategies like deep breathing, progressive muscle relaxation, or mindfulness techniques to ease those racing thoughts and physical tension at bedtime.
- Stimulus Control Therapy: This component focuses on strengthening the connection between your bed and sleep. You'll learn to use your bed only for sleep and sex, and to get out of bed if you can't fall asleep within a set time period.
- Sleep Restriction Therapy: It might sound counterintuitive,

but temporarily limiting the time you spend in bed consolidates your sleep, making it more efficient and less fragmented. As your sleep improves, time in bed is gradually increased.

Why CBT-I is So Effective:

- Targets Root Causes: Unlike sleep medications that might temporarily mask insomnia, CBT-I gets to the heart of the problem, addressing both the mental and behavioral components.
- Long-Lasting Results: CBT-I equips you with coping mechanisms and skills for managing sleep difficulties long after therapy ends.
- No Medication Side Effects: Because it's a non-pharmaceutical approach, you avoid the potential risks and side effects of sleep medications.
- May Help With Other Conditions: Because CBT-I tackles anxiety and worries, it can have benefits beyond insomnia, often improving mood and overall well-being.

CBT-I isn't about immediate results – it's about learning new habits and thought patterns that reshape your relationship with sleep. While it requires effort and consistency, it's one of the most powerful tools in the battle against chronic insomnia. In the next part, we'll discuss when to seek a doctor's evaluation and how to find a qualified sleep therapist.

When to See a Doc and Finding a Therapist

Recognizing that self-help strategies and lifestyle changes aren't enough is a crucial step in reclaiming your sleep. Here are signs it's time to seek professional help:

When to See a Doctor:

- Persistent Struggle: If you consistently have trouble falling asleep, staying asleep, or wake up feeling unrefreshed despite trying good sleep hygiene, a trip to the doctor is crucial.

- Daytime Distress: Chronic sleep deprivation significantly impacts your mood, concentration, productivity, and overall quality of life. A medical evaluation can rule out any underlying causes contributing to your insomnia.
- Suspected Sleep Disorder: Signs like loud snoring, gasping for breath during sleep, excessive daytime sleepiness, or uncontrollable urges to move your legs at night warrant a sleep specialist evaluation.
- Medications Are the Problem: If you suspect a medication you take is interfering with your sleep, discuss alternative options or dosage changes with your doctor.
- Mental Health Concerns: If anxiety, depression, or other mental health conditions are closely intertwined with your sleep problems, seeking treatment for the underlying condition is essential for sleep improvement.

What Your Doctor Might Do:

- Thorough Medical History: Your doctor will ask about your sleep patterns, daytime symptoms, medications, and any health conditions you have.
- Sleep Diary: You may be asked to keep a detailed log of your sleep and wake times, naps, and daytime alertness for a week or two.
- Refer You to a Sleep Specialist: For complex cases or suspected sleep disorders, a referral to a sleep specialist is necessary. Sleep specialists may recommend a sleep study (polysomnography) to monitor your brain waves, breathing, and other vital signs during sleep.

Finding a CBT-I Therapist:

- Seek Qualified Specialists: Look for therapists with specific CBT-I training and expertise. Psychologists, social workers, or counselors can all offer CBT-I if appropriately trained.
- Ask for Referrals: Your doctor, a sleep specialist, or online resources like the Society of Behavioral Sleep Medicine (https://www.behavioralsleep.org/) can provide reputable

referrals.

- Therapy Format: CBT-I can be delivered in individual sessions, group therapy, or occasionally through online programs. Consider what format suits you best.

Don't be afraid to advocate for yourself! If you're struggling with chronic insomnia, there is no shame in seeking help. Remember, asking for support isn't a sign of weakness; it's an act of strength towards better sleep, health, and overall well-being.

SHIFT WORK & SLEEP: A CRUEL MISMATCH

For those who work nights, weekends, or rotating shifts, the struggle for sleep isn't just about bad habits or an overactive mind. It's a biological battle against the very essence of our circadian rhythm. Shift work disrupts the natural alignment of your internal clock with the external light-dark cycle, throwing your body and mind into a state of constant rebellion.

Let's dissect the ways shift work wreaks havoc on sleep:

- Circadian Confusion: Your body craves consistency. Shift work constantly changes the signals your brain receives about when to be awake and when to be asleep. This leads to a state of chronic circadian misalignment.
- Melatonin Mayhem: Light is the primary cue for melatonin suppression or production. Shift workers often sleep during the day (when melatonin should be low) and work under artificial light at night (when melatonin should be rising). This confuses the natural rhythm, making sleep difficult and of poor quality.
- Social Jetlag: Even on "days off," shift workers often struggle to sync their sleep schedule with the rest of the world. This constant feeling of being out of phase with society exacerbates the sleep deprivation and can lead to loneliness and isolation.
- Sleep Time vs. Sleep Quality: Even if you manage to squeeze in enough hours, shift work sleep is often fragmented and less restorative. You might wake up frequently or feel groggy and unrested despite seemingly sufficient time in bed.

The consequences extend far beyond daytime sleepiness:

- Increased Health Risks: Shift work is linked to a higher risk of obesity, diabetes, heart disease, certain types of cancer, and even cognitive decline in the long run. These risks stem from chronic circadian disruption and the unhealthy lifestyle choices that shift work often necessitates.

- Mental Health Impact: Shift work disrupts mood and increases the risk of depression and anxiety. The constant battle against your body's natural inclinations takes a significant toll on mental well-being.
- Impaired Alertness: Fatigue on the job impairs judgment, reaction time, and increases the risk of errors and accidents. This is a danger not only to the shift worker but also to their colleagues and the public.
- Relationship Strain: Working odd hours makes it difficult to maintain social connections and family life. This further exacerbates feelings of isolation and can strain even the strongest relationships.

Does this mean shift workers are doomed to sleep deprivation and its consequences? Absolutely not! While the challenges are undeniable, there are strategies to minimize the impact on sleep patterns. In the next part, we'll delve into coping mechanisms and ways to make shift work a bit less cruel to your sleep.

Strategies for Sleeping Better with Odd Schedules

Surviving, and even thriving, with shift work sleep requires a multifaceted approach. Here's a survival toolkit to combat the challenges:

Strategic Light Exposure: Light is your most powerful tool for manipulating your circadian rhythm. Bright light exposure during your shift can boost alertness, while light-blocking glasses on your way home and blackout curtains in your bedroom can trick your body into believing it's truly nighttime.

Controlled Napping: Short, well-timed naps can combat fatigue without sabotaging nighttime sleep. Aim for 20-30 minute power naps right before your shift or during a scheduled break. Avoid long naps, especially in the latter half of your shift.

Healthy Eating Habits: Shift work often leads to unhealthy eating patterns and reliance on caffeine for artificial energy boosts. Prioritize nutritious meals at regular times as much as possible, limit excessive caffeine before sleep, and have healthy snacks on hand to prevent late-night junk food binges.

Prioritize Sleep on "Days Off": Resist the temptation to completely flip your schedule on days off. While some adjustment is necessary for social activities, aim for a consistent wake-up time even on your days off to minimize circadian disruption.

Create an Ideal Sleep Sanctuary: Your bedroom should be as dark, cool, and quiet as possible, especially if you sleep during the day. Invest in blackout curtains, an eye mask, earplugs, or a white noise machine to create the optimal environment for daytime rest.

Sleep Routine Matters: Even with odd hours, a consistent wind-down routine before bed signals to your brain that it's time to sleep. Avoid screens, have a relaxing bath, or do some light stretches to ease the transition.

Communicate with Loved Ones: Explain the impact of shift work on your sleep and energy levels to your family and friends. Enlist their support in maintaining a quiet environment for you during sleep times and understanding your limitations in terms of social commitments.

Workplace Considerations: If possible, advocate for shift schedules that rotate forward (morning shifts followed by evenings, then nights) as this follows the natural circadian rhythm better. Speak to your supervisor about creating better-lit workspaces and allowing short scheduled breaks for naps on night shifts.

Seek Professional Help: If you struggle despite employing these strategies, talk to your doctor or a sleep specialist. They might recommend light therapy, strategic melatonin use, or treatment for underlying sleep disorders that are exacerbated by shift work.

Remember, even small improvements in sleep quality can make a significant difference in your overall health, well-being, and job performance. While shift work presents unique challenges, understanding your body's rhythms and implementing targeted strategies empowers you to gain a measure of control over your sleep, even in a world that operates on a 9-to-5 schedule.

SPECIAL SLEEP STRUGGLES

Insomnia and Menopause

For women, the battle against insomnia can become even more fierce when menopause enters the picture. The hormonal rollercoaster that accompanies this natural transition disrupts sleep in numerous ways, leaving many women tossing, turning, and desperately craving a full night's rest. Let's unravel why menopause can feel like a sleep-wrecking machine:

Hot Flashes & Night Sweats: One of the most infamous menopause symptoms, these sudden surges of intense heat are a major sleep saboteur. Waking up drenched in sweat, with your heart pounding, disrupts sleep and makes falling back asleep a challenge.

Estrogen's Decline: During menopause, estrogen levels drop. While estrogen's exact role in sleep regulation isn't fully understood, this drop is linked to increased sleep problems and a heightened risk of sleep apnea.

Anxiety & Mood Swings: Hormonal fluctuations can amplify anxiety, lead to mood swings, and low mood – all of which are enemies of restful sleep. The racing thoughts, irritability, and restlessness make it incredibly difficult to relax and drift off.

Other Menopause-Related Sleep Sabotage: Weight gain, which is common during menopause, can increase the risk of sleep apnea. Nighttime bathroom trips due to bladder changes and joint pain due to declining estrogen levels all add to the sleepless nights.

The frustration and exhaustion stemming from chronic sleep deprivation during menopause can make an already challenging time feel even more difficult. Feeling like your own body has turned against you is both physically and emotionally draining.

However, it's important to recognize that sleep struggles are a common part of menopause, and strategies exist to lessen their impact.

In the next part, we'll discuss how to address menopause-induced insomnia, covering both lifestyle changes and potential medical interventions.

Sleep Issues and Aging

Sleep changes as we age. It can become lighter, more fragmented, and those early morning awakenings become more frequent. While some degree of change may be a normal part of aging, debilitating insomnia is not. Let's explore the unique factors that can disrupt sleep for older adults:

Medical Conditions: The prevalence of chronic health conditions like arthritis, heart disease, acid reflux, prostate problems (in men), and overactive bladder increases with age. Pain, discomfort, and frequent nighttime bathroom trips naturally disrupt sleep.

Medication Mayhem: Many older adults take several medications, increasing the risk of sleep-disrupting side effects. Some medications can cause alertness, vivid dreams, or the need for nighttime urination.

Weakened Circadian Rhythm: As we age, our internal clock becomes less robust. This can lead to earlier sleep onset and earlier wake-up times, making it harder to maintain a "normal" sleep schedule if life responsibilities or social engagements require later bedtimes.

Insomnia-Worsening Habits: Changes like retirement and reduced physical activity can lead to less structured daytime routines. Long daytime naps, excessive caffeine use, and spending more time in bed awake can all exacerbate insomnia.

Anxiety, Depression, and Grief: Older adults can face unique stressors, including loneliness, concerns about health, loss of loved ones, and worries about the future. Mental health struggles significantly impact sleep quality.

Sleep Disorders on the Rise: The risk of sleep disorders like sleep apnea, restless legs syndrome, and REM sleep behavior disorder increases with age. These disorders cause significant sleep disruption and require medical diagnosis and treatment.

Managing Sleep Struggles as We Age:

- Talk to Your Doctor: A thorough evaluation to rule out or manage underlying medical conditions and a review of all your medications is crucial. Addressing the root cause is the first step towards better sleep.
- Sleep Hygiene Matters: Even more so with age, a consistent sleep-wake schedule, a sleep-conducive bedroom, avoiding daytime naps, and strategic use of light exposure are essential.
- Managing Anxiety & Mood: Seek help for anxiety or depression. Cognitive Behavioral Therapy (including CBT-I for insomnia), relaxation techniques, or medication might be necessary to improve both mental well-being and sleep.
- Timed Exercise: Regular physical activity promotes better sleep, but avoid intense exercise too close to bedtime. Morning or afternoon workouts are ideal for most older adults.
- Cognitive Stimulation: Keeping your mind active with hobbies, puzzles, and social activities can indirectly improve sleep by reducing daytime napping and lessening nighttime boredom or worry.

It's important for both older adults and their loved ones to remember: Sleep struggles are not inevitable. Seeking help when sleep deprivation becomes significant is essential for improving quality of life and overall health.

THE SLEEP/MENTAL HEALTH CONNECTION

Insomnia as a Symptom of Depression or Anxiety Disorders

The relationship between sleep and mental health is a complex, two-way street. Insomnia isn't just a nuisance; it can be a red flag signaling underlying depression, anxiety, or other mental health conditions. Let's unravel the deep connections:

Insomnia: A Core Symptom: Difficulty falling asleep, staying asleep, and early-morning awakenings are common symptoms of depression. Disrupted sleep can also be one of the earliest signs of a change in mood.

Generalized Anxiety Disorder (GAD): Characterized by excessive worry and tension, GAD makes turning off racing thoughts at bedtime nearly impossible. The anticipatory anxiety about *not* sleeping further intensifies the cycle.

Panic Disorder: Nighttime panic attacks can jolt you awake, heart pounding and fear overwhelming. The aftermath leaves you hypervigilant and afraid to fall back asleep.

Post-Traumatic Stress Disorder (PTSD): Disturbing flashbacks, nightmares, and hyperarousal associated with PTSD make sleep feel unsafe and fragmented. Waking with a jolt in a sweat-soaked bed is a common, nightmarish experience.

Bipolar Disorder: Sleep disturbances are present in both manic and depressive phases of Bipolar disorder. Mania can lead to drastically reduced need for sleep, while depression often comes with hypersomnia (excessive sleeping) or severe insomnia.

When Mental Illness Causes the Sleeplessness:

- Disordered Thinking: Depressive rumination, racing anxious thoughts, or the intrusive thoughts that accompany PTSD all keep your mind in overdrive – the opposite of what you need for sleep.

- Changes in Brain Chemistry: The neurotransmitters involved in regulating sleep, like serotonin and norepinephrine, are also implicated in mood disorders. Disruptions in these systems impact both mood and sleep regulation.
- Hyperarousal: Anxiety disorders put your body in a constant state of fight-or-flight, making it incredibly difficult to reach the relaxed, parasympathetic state needed for sleep.

The negative consequences of this are substantial. Chronic sleep deprivation worsens mood, makes anxiety harder to manage, increases risk for relapse in depressive episodes, and reduces your ability to cope with the challenges that mental illness presents.

How Better Sleep Can Improve Overall Well-Being

The good news is that the relationship between sleep and mental health isn't a one-way street of doom. Improving sleep can have profound positive impacts on mood, resilience, and overall mental well-being. Here's how:

Reduced Anxiety: Getting adequate sleep allows your brain and body to recover from the daily stresses. This translates to better emotional regulation, decreased irritability, and an increased ability to handle anxiety-provoking situations.

Improved Mood: While good sleep won't cure depression, it's a crucial component of managing it. Restedness allows for clearer thinking, better coping skills, and less emotional reactivity.

Enhanced Focus & Concentration: Sleep deprivation impairs attention, memory, and decision-making – all of which are essential for managing mental health challenges. Improved sleep translates to better cognitive function and a greater sense of control.

Increased Resilience: When you're well-rested, you have more mental energy to face challenges, engage in therapy effectively, and utilize healthy coping mechanisms.

Boosted Motivation: One of the hallmarks of depression is a lack of motivation. While sleep won't magically bring it back, better sleep means less debilitating fatigue, making it easier to engage in activities that foster a sense of purpose and well-being.

The Virtuous Cycle Begins: Improving sleep, even slightly, can create positive momentum. Feeling more rested improves mood, which boosts motivation for good sleep hygiene practices, leading to further sleep improvement.

How to Target the Sleep-Mental Health Link:

- Seek Professional Help: If you notice a strong connection between your sleep struggles and mental health, seek evaluation and treatment from a qualified mental health professional.
- Prioritize Sleep Hygiene: Good sleep hygiene habits are essential, even in the face of mental health challenges. While they might not solve everything, they form a strong foundation.
- CBT-I for the Win: Cognitive Behavioral Therapy for Insomnia is often incredibly effective for people with mental health conditions, addressing both the insomnia and the underlying thought patterns that worsen both sleep and mood.
- Address the Root Cause: Treating the underlying depression, anxiety, or PTSD is crucial for long-term improvement. Medication, targeted therapy, and lifestyle changes can be integral parts of treatment.

Remember, the sleep-mental health connection is complex. Don't expect overnight miracles – improving sleep takes time and effort. But each night of better sleep is an investment in your overall well-being, strengthening your mental and emotional resilience for the challenges ahead.

WEIRD BUT TRUE: UNCOMMON SLEEP DISORDERS

We tend to think of sleep disorders as confined to insomnia, snoring, or the occasional bout of sleepwalking. However, the world of sleep can be far stranger and more disruptive than we might expect. Let's explore some of the less common but incredibly fascinating sleep disorders:

Restless Legs Syndrome (RLS): More than just an annoyance, RLS is a neurological disorder marked by a powerful, almost irresistible urge to move your legs. This is accompanied by crawling, tingling, burning, or other deeply unpleasant sensations. These symptoms primarily occur at night and when at rest, making falling asleep extraordinarily difficult.

Sleep Apnea: Obstructive sleep apnea (OSA) is a potentially serious condition. It occurs when the airway repeatedly collapses during sleep, causing pauses in breathing. This leads to fragmented sleep, snoring, and daytime exhaustion. OSA increases the risk of heart disease, stroke, and other health problems if left untreated.

Narcolepsy: Often portrayed comically in movies, narcolepsy is a chronic disorder characterized by excessive daytime sleepiness, even with adequate nighttime sleep. Cataplexy (sudden muscle weakness triggered by strong emotions), vivid hallucinations while falling asleep, and sleep paralysis can be debilitating symptoms.

REM Sleep Behavior Disorder (RBD): In RBD, the normal muscle paralysis that occurs during REM sleep (when we dream most vividly) is lost. People act out their dreams with movements, talking, yelling, or even violent thrashing and punching. This can lead to self-injury or injury to their bed partner.

Night Terrors: Unlike nightmares, night terrors occur during deep sleep and involve intense feelings of terror or dread, screaming, thrashing, and rapid heartbeat. The person is usually difficult to wake and has no memory of the event upon awakening. Night terrors are more common in children, but can persist into adulthood.

Sleepwalking (Somnambulism): Ranging from simply sitting up in bed to complex actions like walking around, eating, or even driving, sleepwalking occurs during deep sleep. The sleepwalker is usually unaware of their actions and has no recall afterwards.

Why Understanding Uncommon Disorders Matters:

- You're Not Alone: Realizing your bizarre sleep struggles have a name and are an acknowledged medical condition can be incredibly validating. Often these disorders get misdiagnosed, leading to frustration and unnecessary suffering.
- Seeking Specialized Help: Correct diagnosis is crucial for getting the right treatment. A sleep specialist can order tests like a polysomnography (sleep study) to pinpoint the problem and devise an appropriate treatment plan.
- Potential for Relief: Many uncommon sleep disorders can be effectively managed with medication, therapy (like CBT for nightmares), or safety precautions. While not always curable, regaining a sense of control and improving sleep quality can be life-changing.

If you experience chronically unrefreshing sleep with any of the strange or disruptive symptoms described, don't dismiss them as simply "weird." Talk to your doctor or seek a referral to a sleep specialist. Delving into the world of uncommon sleep disorders might illuminate your path towards diagnosis, treatment, and finally, the restful nights you deserve.

When Insomnia is a Sign of Something More Serious

Sometimes, what seems like chronic insomnia is actually a red flag signaling a serious, and possibly overlooked, medical condition. While less common, it's important to be aware of these potential culprits:

- Neurological Diseases: Parkinson's Disease, dementia, and other neurological conditions can significantly disrupt sleep patterns. Sleep fragmentation, vivid dreams, acting out dreams, and daytime sleepiness can be early manifestations of these diseases.

- Hyperthyroidism: An overactive thyroid can cause a state of hyperarousal, with a racing heart and restlessness that makes sleep incredibly difficult. Other symptoms like weight loss, anxiety, and heat intolerance might provide clues.

- Chronic Pain Conditions: The discomfort associated with conditions like fibromyalgia, arthritis, or chronic back pain can obviously interfere with sleep. The pain itself and the mental stress it causes creates a vicious cycle of worsened sleep and intensified pain.

- Certain Medications: Some medications, including certain antidepressants, steroids, and blood pressure medications, are notorious for disrupting sleep. If your sleep struggles began after starting a new medication, investigating this angle with your doctor is crucial.

- Sleep-Related Movement Disorders: These are less well-known but can cause chronic sleep disruption. Periodic Limb Movement Disorder (PLMD) involves repetitive twitching or jerking of the legs during sleep, often unnoticed by the sleeper themselves, but can lead to frequent arousals.

Why Awareness Matters:

- Earlier Diagnosis, Better Treatment: Untreated medical conditions tend to worsen over time. Identifying the underlying cause is the first step towards managing the condition itself and hopefully improving sleep in the process.

- Avoiding the Misdiagnosis Trap: Simply being handed a sleep medication prescription without a thorough evaluation risks missing a potentially treatable condition and prolonging the sleep struggle unnecessarily.
- Tailored Treatment: Treating the underlying cause often offers better long-term management than solely relying on sleep aids. Improved sleep might be a fantastic side effect of addressing the main medical issue.

When to Push for Further Investigation:

- Recent Changes: If your sleep patterns drastically worsen within a short time frame, unexplained by stress or obvious lifestyle culprits, seek medical evaluation.
- Atypical Insomnia Symptoms: If your insomnia is accompanied by daytime sleepiness, unusual movements during sleep, or other concerning daytime symptoms like tremors, unintended weight loss, or cognitive changes, a thorough medical workup is necessary.
- Gut Feeling: If you have a nagging feeling that something else is amiss even if your doctor initially dismisses it, trust your instincts. Seek a second opinion or ask for a referral to a specialist to rule out underlying medical causes of your sleep troubles.

Remember, being your own advocate is an essential component of achieving better health and ultimately, better sleep.

BEYOND PILLS: ALTERNATIVE SLEEP THERAPIES

While medication can be a helpful tool for addressing sleep issues in certain situations, it's far from the only solution. There's a growing interest in alternative and complementary approaches to manage insomnia. Let's explore some potentially helpful options, always remembering the importance of consulting your healthcare provider before trying any new therapy.

Acupuncture for Better Sleep? The Jury's Still Out: This ancient Chinese practice involves inserting thin needles into specific acupoints on the body. Some studies suggest potential benefits for insomnia, possibly by influencing the release of sleep-regulating neurotransmitters. However, research is limited and results can be individual. Acupuncture is generally safe when performed by a licensed professional but might not be the magic bullet for everyone.

Weighted Blankets: The Deep Pressure Touch: These heavy blankets provide deep pressure stimulation, thought to have a calming effect by increasing serotonin and melatonin levels. While more research is needed, some people with insomnia, anxiety, or sensory processing issues find them incredibly comforting, promoting a sense of security that aids in sleep. It's important to choose the right weight for your body size and avoid them if you have respiratory problems or circulation issues.

Yoga Nidra for Deep Relaxation: This guided meditation practice focuses on cultivating a state of deep relaxation between waking and sleeping. It can be incredibly effective for reducing stress, calming racing thoughts, and easing the transition into sleep. Yoga Nidra can be found in classes, guided recordings, or apps specifically for sleep.

Progressive Muscle Relaxation (PMR): A technique where you systematically tense and release different muscle groups throughout the body. This promotes body awareness and reduces physical tension, both of which can be major barriers to sleep, especially when anxiety is a factor.

The Potential of Hypnotherapy: While often associated with stage performances, clinical hypnotherapy uses guided relaxation, focused attention, and suggestion to address a variety of concerns, including insomnia. Research in this area is limited, and finding a reputable hypnotherapist is key. This might be more beneficial for those who are highly suggestible.

Important Considerations with Alternative Therapies:

- Not One-Size-Fits-All: What works wonders for one person might do nothing for another. It's essential to manage expectations and approach alternative therapies with an open yet critical mind.
- Best as Part of the Puzzle: Alternative therapies often work best alongside good sleep hygiene practices, relaxation techniques, and therapy to address underlying anxiety or thought patterns fueling your insomnia.
- Do Your Homework: Research the therapy you're interested in, look for reputable practitioners with experience in addressing sleep issues, and always inform your doctor before starting any new approach.

While alternative therapies might not provide immediate insomnia cures, they can offer valuable tools to calm your mind, reduce tension, and enhance a sense of well-being that indirectly supports healthier sleep patterns.

Can Weighted Blankets or Light Therapy Help?

Let's delve into two alternative therapies that warrant a closer look, both with some scientific backing, but also some important caveats:

Weighted Blankets: More Than Just a Trend

The science behind the hype: There's a growing body of research suggesting that the deep pressure stimulation provided by weighted blankets can:

- Increase "feel good" chemicals: Studies show an increase in serotonin (a mood stabilizer) and melatonin (the sleep-promoting hormone), while reducing cortisol (the stress hormone).
- Promote Relaxation: Deep touch pressure may activate the parasympathetic nervous system, responsible for our "rest and digest" state, counteracting the hyperarousal that keeps insomniacs awake.
- Offer Comfort & Security: For some, the weight of the blanket feels similar to a comforting hug, providing a sense of security that reduces anxiety and promotes a sense of calm.

Who might benefit: While not a cure-all, weighted blankets may be particularly helpful for those with:

- Anxiety: The calming pressure can ease the physical symptoms of anxiety, quieting a racing mind and promoting relaxation.
- Sensory Processing Issues: Individuals with autism or sensory sensitivities often find the deep pressure input soothing and regulating.
- Restless Legs Syndrome: Some people with RLS report a reduction in the intensity of the unpleasant sensations.

Important Considerations:

- Blanket Weight Matters: Aim for a blanket that's about 10% of your body weight. Too heavy can feel restrictive or make you overheat.
- Cost Factor: Weighted blankets can be expensive, so consider trying a lighter "test" blanket with added weights before

investing in a heavier one.

- **Not for Everyone:** Avoid weighted blankets if you have sleep apnea, respiratory issues, or circulation problems. They might not be suitable if you get overheated easily or feel claustrophobic.

Light Therapy: Harnessing the Power of Light

The Concept: Bright light therapy, typically using a specialized light box, aims to regulate your circadian rhythm. It's based on the principle that light is the most powerful cue for suppressing melatonin and promoting alertness.

How it's used for sleep issues:

- Shifting Sleep Schedules: Strategically timed light exposure can help adjust your internal clock, useful for delayed sleep phase syndrome, jet lag, or shift work.
- Seasonal Affective Disorder (SAD): For SAD, characterized by depression brought on by reduced daylight in winter, light therapy can improve mood and indirectly aid sleep.

Promising, But Not a Panacea: Light therapy, when used correctly, can be helpful for specific sleep issues. However, it's not a universal insomnia fix. It's essential to get a proper diagnosis and consult a doctor for appropriate use and timing of light therapy, as incorrect use can worsen sleep problems.

Alternative therapies hold potential, but they are not a replacement for seeking medical advice and addressing the root causes of your insomnia. They work best when integrated into a holistic approach that prioritizes healthy sleep habits, stress management, and treatment of any underlying health issues contributing to your sleep struggles.

TRAVEL & SLEEP: A JET-LAGGED NIGHTMARE

Travel, with its disruptions to routine and time zone changes, can wreak havoc on your sleep. Even a short trip can leave you tossing and turning, feeling drained instead of rejuvenated. Let's break down why travel is often the enemy of good sleep and explore strategies to minimize its disruptive effects.

The Jet Lag Culprit: Your Circadian Rhythm is Confused: Your internal clock is stubbornly set to your home time zone. When you rapidly cross multiple time zones, your body's perception of day and night is completely out of sync with the local time. This leads to sleepiness when you should be awake, difficulty falling asleep at the appropriate bedtime, and that disorienting feeling of being out of sorts.

Travel Fatigue Adds to the Misery: Cramped airplane seats, long hours in transit, irregular eating schedules, and dehydration all contribute to general fatigue. This compounds the sleep issues caused by jet lag, leaving you feeling physically and mentally exhausted.

Unfamiliar Surroundings: A new hotel room, strange noises, an uncomfortable bed – these changes to your sleep environment can make it harder to drift off. The lack of familiar cues and comforts disrupts your sense of security.

Excitement or Anxiety: Whether it's the anticipation of a vacation or the stress of a business trip, the mental stimulation associated with travel can keep your mind buzzing, making relaxing for sleep a challenge.

The Consequences of Travel-Induced Sleep Deprivation:

- Daytime Drowsiness: Impaired alertness and concentration

make sightseeing, conducting business, or just enjoying your trip difficult and potentially unsafe.

- Crankiness & Mood Swings: Sleep deprivation makes you a less pleasant version of yourself, impacting relationships with travel companions.
- Weakened Immunity: Getting sick while traveling is the worst! Lack of sleep compromises your immune function, increasing your susceptibility to catching bugs.
- Worsens Existing Sleep Issues: For anyone with chronic insomnia, travel can exacerbate the problem, making sleep even more elusive.

While jet lag might seem like an inevitable travel woe, you're not completely at its mercy! In the next part, we'll discuss strategies to minimize sleep disruptions and make your travels less exhausting.

Tips for Minimizing Disruption When Time Zones Change

Pre-Trip Preparation:

- Gradual Adjustment: If possible, start shifting your sleep and wake times a few days before your trip, moving them closer to the destination time zone. Even small adjustments can help.
- Hydrate & Nourish: In the days leading up to your departure, prioritize good hydration and healthy, balanced meals. This helps counteract in-flight dehydration and irregular eating schedules.
- Sleep Well Beforehand: Being sleep-deprived before you leave only amplifies the effects of jet lag. Prioritize good rest in the nights leading up to your trip.

During Your Travels:

- Strategic Napping: If you arrive exhausted, a short (20-30 minutes) early-afternoon nap can provide a temporary boost. Avoid long naps or napping too late in the day, as this worsens nighttime sleep struggles.

- Timed Light Exposure: Seek sunlight upon arrival to help reset your circadian rhythm. If you arrive at night, avoid bright light and use blackout curtains to create darkness.
- Be Active, But Not Too Late: Light to moderate exercise during the day can combat fatigue, but avoid intense exercise close to your desired bedtime, as it can be stimulating.
- Stay Hydrated: Dehydration worsens jet lag symptoms. Drink plenty of water throughout your flight and upon arrival.
- Limit Alcohol & Caffeine: These substances throw your sleep off further. Minimize them, especially in the days after arrival when your body is adjusting.

At Your Destination:

- Embrace Local Time: As tempting as it is to cling to your home time zone, resist! Eat meals at local times, and try to align your sleep-wake schedule with the new time zone as quickly as possible.
- Melatonin Might Help: A short-term, low-dose melatonin supplement, taken in the evening at your destination's bedtime, has some evidence for aiding with the sleep-wake shift. However, consult your doctor before using and note that timing and dosage are crucial.
- A Comfortable Space: Request a quiet hotel room, use your travel pillow and eye mask, and pack any other comforts that help create a sleep-friendly environment.
- Consider Medication...Cautiously: For severe jet lag or crucial events upon arrival, talk to your doctor about the possibility of a short-acting sleep aid for a few nights only. However, sleeping pills have risks and shouldn't be relied on regularly.

Listen to Your Body: Be patient. Your body needs time to adjust to the new time zone. Rest when you need to, but resist the urge to sleep too much during the day.

It's important to have realistic expectations. Some degree of jet lag may be unavoidable, particularly with long flights crossing multiple time zones. However, by implementing these strategies, you can lessen the severity of sleep disruption and recover from jet lag more quickly, making your travel adventures more enjoyable and less fraught with sleepless nights.

REAL-LIFE INSOMNIACS: SUCCESS STORIES

After chapters of analyzing sleep problems and strategies, it's time to inject some inspiration. Real-life success stories illustrate that overcoming insomnia, while rarely easy, is absolutely possible. These stories provide valuable insights into what works and offer a much-needed dose of hope for those struggling with chronic sleeplessness.

Story 1: Sarah - Breaking Free from the Medication Trap

Sarah, a middle-aged woman, had relied on sleep medication for years. Initially, it felt like a lifesaver, but gradually the drugs lost effectiveness, leaving her groggy and dependent on them for the faintest hope of a decent night. Fearful but determined, she worked with a therapist specializing in CBT-I. It wasn't easy – she faced restless nights and intense withdrawal symptoms. However, she learned to change her thoughts about sleep, employed relaxation techniques to calm her anxiety, and practiced the sleep restriction strategies that felt counterintuitive at first. Slowly, her sleep became less reliant on pills and more responsive to the healthy habits she'd cultivated. It wasn't perfect sleep, but it was *her* sleep, and that felt empowering.

Story 2: Jason - Conquering Sleep Apnea and Reclaiming His Energy

Jason attributed his daytime exhaustion and persistent insomnia to stress and a busy lifestyle. Prodding from his concerned wife led him to a sleep study. The diagnosis of severe sleep apnea came as a shock. Adjusting to a CPAP machine was awkward, but the difference was night and day (literally!). The fog of fatigue lifted, sleep was more restful, and even chronic insomnia improved. He realized that a hidden medical culprit had been sabotaging his sleep all along.

Story 3: Emily - Taming the Racing Mind

Emily's mind was a relentless thought factory at night, replaying worries and dissecting past events. Guided meditation was a game-changer. Initially it felt silly to focus on her breath, but with consistent practice, she gained the ability to observe her anxious thoughts without getting swept away in them. Journaling helped to get the worries out of her head before bed. Sleep wasn't instantly transformed, but the hyper-alertness that fueled her insomnia gradually softened. She learned that a calm mind creates space for sleep.

Key Themes in these Stories:

- It's a Process, Not a Miracle: Conquering insomnia takes time and effort. There are setbacks and frustrating nights, but perseverance towards healthier sleep pays off.
- Multifaceted Approach: Success often involves a combination of strategies – changing thoughts and behaviors, addressing underlying anxiety, improving sleep hygiene, or sometimes, getting the right medical treatment.
- Small Victories Matter: Celebrating even incremental improvements in sleep quality and energy levels fuels motivation.
- There is Hope: Hearing that others have emerged from the exhaustion of chronic sleeplessness offers the most important ingredient for anyone struggling with insomnia – hope.

Finding the Strategies That Work for *You*

Inspired by these success stories but wondering where to start? Remember, the path to better sleep is individual. Here's the takeaway from real-life successes and how to tailor your own approach:

The Power of a Thorough Evaluation: Before anything else, rule out medical causes for your insomnia, especially if you experience snoring, daytime sleepiness, or other unusual symptoms. Don't assume all sleep struggles are due to simple bad habits.

Embrace Experimentation: What transformed Emily's sleep might do little for Sarah, and vice-versa. Be willing to try various strategies. Keep a sleep journal to track what helps, what doesn't, and notice how your body and mind respond to different approaches.

Professional Guidance: A therapist specializing in CBT-I can be invaluable for navigating the behavioral and psychological aspects of insomnia, particularly when anxiety is a major player.

Realistic Expectations: Don't aim for perfect sleep every single night. Good sleep habits and insomnia management techniques make "bad nights" less frequent and less devastating.

Focus on Progress, Not Perfection: Did you manage to fall asleep a little faster? Did you wake up slightly less frequently? Did you have a day with more energy than usual? Celebrate those wins! They are stepping stones to more consistent improvement.

Build Your Sleep Toolkit: Even when sleep improves, stressful periods or life changes can provoke temporary disruptions. Having a toolkit of techniques – relaxation strategies, sleep hygiene adjustments, ways to calm racing thoughts – empowers you to regain control quickly.

Don't Give Up: Some improvement might happen relatively quickly, while other aspects of sleep may take longer to shift. Remember those success stories – if others could overcome their relentless insomnia, so can you.

Inspiration Fuels Action: Reading about positive outcomes empowers you to take action towards better sleep. Whether it's experimenting with a calming bedtime routine, scheduling that doctor's appointment, or researching therapists who specialize in sleep, these success stories highlight that insomnia doesn't have to be your forever reality.

THE JOY OF SLEEP REDISCOVERED

Picture this: Instead of hitting the pillow and bracing for another sleepless night, you approach bedtime with a sense of calm anticipation. Your bedroom feels like an inviting sanctuary. You drift off without a struggle, wake up less frequently during the night, and awaken feeling genuinely rested for the first time in ages. This newfound relationship with sleep has a ripple effect throughout your life.

The Benefits of Restorative Sleep:

- Energy Recharged: You are no longer a slave to your exhaustion. Simple tasks don't feel like insurmountable hurdles, and you might even (gasp!) have the energy to exercise or pick up a forgotten hobby.
- Sharper Mind: The brain fog dissipates. You think more clearly, problem-solving becomes easier, and those embarrassing moments of forgetting simple words become less frequent.
- Emotional Regulation: Irritability and mood swings lessen. You have the reserves to handle stress and setbacks without immediately collapsing into despair or snapping at loved ones.
- Improved Health: Chronic sleep deprivation is linked to scary health risks. Better sleep strengthens your immune system and supports your overall physical well-being.
- A Happier You: When you're not exhausted all the time, you rediscover joy in daily life. Relationships improve, you're more engaged in activities, and a sense of optimism and possibility re-emerges.

Sleep as a Part of Self-Care:

Overcoming insomnia often necessitates lifestyle shifts. Instead of seeing these as sacrifices, view them as prioritizing a fundamental aspect of your well-being:

- Regularity Matters: A consistent sleep-wake schedule trains your body and mind to expect sleep at a certain time, creating powerful cues for restfulness.
- Movement is Key: Regular exercise (but not too close to bedtime) makes a profound difference in sleep quality. Even a short walk is better than no activity.
- Mindfulness: Whether it's a few minutes of meditation, a calming walk in nature, or simply a relaxing bath before bed, carve out time to calm your mind and ease yourself into a state conducive to sleep.
- Nourish Your Body: A healthy diet supports healthy sleep. Avoid heavy late-night meals, limit excessive caffeine and alcohol, and consider whether food sensitivities might be playing a role in your sleep disruptions.

These changes aren't just about fixing insomnia. They represent a commitment to overall health and well-being, with the reward of better sleep as a powerful motivator.

Maintaining Your Newfound Sleep Rhythm

The journey to better sleep doesn't end the moment you have a few decent nights, It's an ongoing process of safeguarding your hard-won improvements. Here's how to make this newfound healthy sleep pattern a lasting habit:

Flexibility Within Routine: Life happens. While a consistent schedule is key, don't panic if you temporarily have to deviate. Get back on track as soon as possible, and don't allow one late night to derail your entire routine.

Anticipate Setbacks: Stressful events, illness, or travel can disrupt your sleep. This is normal! Use your sleep toolkit to navigate these periods. The gentler you are with yourself, the quicker you can bounce back from temporary disruptions.

Don't Fear the Occasional Bad Night: Everyone experiences restless nights from time to time. Instead of spiraling into insomnia anxiety, remind yourself that you have the skills to cope. Focus on good sleep practices the next day to reset your rhythm.

Re-evaluate as Needed: If you find sleep problems creeping back in, don't hesitate to revisit your strategies or seek additional help. Maybe your light-blocking curtains aren't adequate anymore. Perhaps a new stressor in your life necessitates a renewed focus on relaxation techniques.

Celebrate Your Success: Actively acknowledge how much better your life is with consistent, restful sleep. This reinforces your motivation to maintain the good habits that got you here and fuels your determination to address new sleep obstacles as they inevitably arise.

The Empowering Legacy of Your Insomnia Battle:

Overcoming insomnia isn't just about the sleep itself; it's about discovering the power you have over your well-being. You learn:

- Self-Advocacy: Seeking the right help, whether that's from doctors, therapists, or through your own research, fosters a powerful sense of agency over your health.
- Resilience: Facing the frustration of sleeplessness and continuing to try new approaches builds inner strength and resilience that extends to other areas of life.
- The Mind-Body Connection: You gain a deep understanding of how thoughts, behaviors, and your environment intricately impact your sleep. This awareness empowers you to make positive choices for your health far beyond the bedroom.

The pages of this book have addressed the complexities of insomnia, explored solutions, and offered a guiding hand on the path towards better sleep. However, the most important part of this journey is *yours*. Take the knowledge and strategies you've gained and apply them to your unique circumstances. Experiment, be patient with yourself, celebrate victories, and never lose sight of the profoundly restorative power of a good night's sleep.

May this book be not just a collection of words, but a catalyst for a transformation – a transformation that leads you from sleepless nights and weary days to the rediscovery of rest, rejuvenation, and the joy that comes with feeling like your best self again.